Embracing the Sky

Embracing the Sky
Poems beyond Disability

Craig Romkema

Jessica Kingsley Publishers
London and Philadelphia

The right of Craig Romkema to be identified as author of this work has been asserted by him in accordance with the Copyright, Designs and Patents Act 1988

First published in the United Kingdom in 2002
by Jessica Kingsley Publishers Ltd
116 Pentonville Road
London N1 9JB, England
and
325 Chestnut Street
Philadelphia, PA 19106, USA

www.jkp.com

Copyright © Craig Romkema 2002

Library of Congress Cataloging in Publication Data
A CIP catalog record for this book is available from the Library of Congress

British Library Cataloguing in Publication Data
A CIP catalogue record for this book is available from the British Library

ISBN 1 84310 728 7

Printed and Bound in Great Britain by
Athenaeum Press, Gateshead, Tyne and Wear

For my dad
who never gave up,
my mom,
of course,
my siblings
who live with the effects,
and all of you
who share my life…
blessings and hope.

Contents

Nightmare

Mornings are the worst,
Unfolding the stiff ball of my numb body,
Opening my eyes to another twelve hours
Or so of living inside
This shell,
My enemy as well as my friend,
My rocking, waving, throbbing, grinding companion,
My only contact with life.
Sometimes at night, when I lay in
My cocoon of blankets and darkness,
I imagine what I might have looked like,
Been like, the other way,
Without whatever virus or injury caused all of this.
Would I have been considered handsome?
A good match for some beautiful woman?
Would my legs have carried me
To the State Track Championship
As my father's did?
Would people have elected me to societies
And wanted me for a prom date?
Would they have marveled at my creativity and
        intelligence
Instead of expecting me to prove them
Over and over again?
Just a little thing in my system,
Some glitch makes all the difference.
Sometimes I lay there wishing
This was all a bad dream.

But morning comes
And I am grateful for one finger that types,
One school that lets me in,
And someone patient enough
To bear it all with me.

Heaven can't come fast enough some days.

Dedication

Giving up is a non-option,
personal backtracking into
the womb of silence and strangulation.
I have tasted both worlds now
and although I can do without
your ear-splitting jangle of progressiveness,
ninety miles an hour,
no rest stops ahead,
I cannot resist the daily unfolding
of one spirit to another,
word-bonding, truth-sharing,
verifying life.
Addicting explorations engage the guru mind,
but you and I exchange
mind's wisdom, heart's affection,
spirit's honor.
In each new friend's eyes I have fathomed
knowledge only accessible
through your world's currency—
words piled on words,
libraries of words,
so I am using your connecting force
to describe my journey,
one letter at a time,
two phrases,
a family of observations,
this volume.

I dare not do otherwise
for we need
each other.

Impatience

I listen to their bickering about
Who has to do the dishes
And wonder if I'll ever be able
To finish a sinkful alone.
Movement disorder they call it—
Difficulty stopping, starting, continuing
Motion.
One of the great challenges
Of my life.
Give me wrist support
And I can write a story,
Touch my back
And I can walk smoothly down the hall,
Hum to me
And I can keep going and going
And going,
Take away these supports
And I may be frozen,
Jerky, silent.
A doctor out East may have the answer—
Two parts of the brain missing their connection.
Maybe someday a computer chip
Can regulate my body,
Imbedded in my brain
Like a gift from heaven.
Until then I listen to them bickering…
And wait for my turn to scrub.

Riding Lesson

He sniffs my palm;
I wince.
This brown horse I'm supposed
to climb on
shortly,
is gentle, they say,
as they guide my hand in
brushing his quivering neck.
They lead us both out to the ring.
I climb the platform,
then feel strong arms half-lifting
my rebellious legs over
Ace's back,
while he stands patiently,
waiting.

Airborne,
with horseflesh between my thighs,
I can't figure out
where to hold on
or how to keep my back
from swaying
after every step.

Dazzling lights make patterns on
the red dusty ground;
next door a windmill spins,

pulling my eyes into
its vortex.
Volunteers stride silently,
occasionally calling encouragement,
their voices blending with
crickets
and the squeak of leather.

We make one round,
two,
as I settle into the rhythm
of this animal's gait.
I wonder how he tolerates
saddle and bridle
and human
weighing him down.

We move together
wordlessly,
man and creature sensing
each other.

Then they lead us home,
stable-bound,
slide me down his side
to solid earth;
I breathe deeply
horse-leather-hay
and stumble out
into the night.

The Dance Of Language

They were my first entering-point
into life,
not the life of horrifyingly-loud sirens,
or scratchy clothes,
or food too frustratingly-distasteful to touch.
That was only withdrawing from great pain,
from what was forced upon me.
How could I know that others didn't experience
life this way?

It was the words that showed me.
I don't know where understanding begins,
but it was there.
I found it in the stories people read to me,
in the rhythms of poetry, and the dance of language,
I found comfort,
and soon the words began to explain
the chaos of my life
and I knew that I was loved.

I figured out that people liked
many things I hated,
that food and clothes were part
of everyone's existence.
Peter Rabbit and The Runaway Bunny loved them;
I was alone in finding them unbearable.
The stories explained that my experience
was strange,

and in the book, *The Beast*,
I saw it all.
I carried that book around with me for weeks,
and cried when it was read to me,
because Robert, Reba, and Raymond thought they
    knew
the Beast.
They thought he was ferocious
and should be killed,
but Anna was the only one,
who knew the Beast at all.
I was the Beast.
All the loving people who
tried to reach me were Anna.

The words fascinate me, terrify
and excite me.
In their black-and-white patterns they capture
life, love, hatred, empathy,
all the great stuff of our emotions.
I collect words in my mind,
like jewels on a silk cord.
I bring them out for display, then hide
them again.
Words were my answer to sensation's questions.
They are my delight, to share with you.
For your questions.
For your answers.

Transition

Where does the boy-fascination end
and autism begin?
I never played with cars,
just watched my brother's eyes light up
with every passing tractor, truck,
Hummer, lawn-mower, machine,
listened to him spout statistics about
models, engines, parts.
For me, the sounds were addicting,
the fantasy of power.
He thrums-thrums-thrums his way up and
down the stairs,
while I listen,
entranced by
comrade-love of reverberating engines,
pumping pistons.
He doesn't know I make the sounds
inside my head,
as fighter pilot roaring
through piles of clouds,
or motorcycle rider gunning my way
past semis spewing exhaust.
So where does the autism begin?
My eyes and hands don't coalesce
with voice and courage enough
to play with him.
I play alone with sound,
sticking paper and objects in

bicycle wheels,
spinning, listening,
spinning again.
I work with what I can,
play with what I can.
So does he.
Again I ask you,
Are we both simply living within
the scope of our
opportunities?
Is that where autism begins?

The Dilemma

Reason shouts its easy triumph!
"There is nothing holding you
To the behaviors
That rule your every minute."
Now they creep back,
Teasing me,
Daring me
To loose their stranglehold over my mind and body.
Babbling tapes keep my mouth busy,
Others confused;
Only the typing hand gives me a way out.
I want to fight, but how?
The behaviors are the clothes I wear.
I am not ready to be alone,
And naked.

Declaration

The glance
ricocheting into thought,
assaying my appearance,
combined with misperceptions
about people like
us.

I am here beside you
thinking, learning,
dreaming,
while my body,
like some freakish
other self,
carries out ridiculous
contortions,
silly games,
rubbish routines,
which you see,

And I see
the glance,
disbelief reflected
in your eyes
leading to
stress,
further craziness,
isolation.

I am
not my body.

I am
not my autism.

I am.

Perspectives

Doing nothing down in my room,
I lie on my bed watching the fluttering
of a pen between my incessant fingers.
Self-stimulation, some experts call this,
eastern mystics might consider it meditating,
psychologists used to blame it
on "refrigerator mothers",
optometrists prescribe special exercises and glasses,
researchers recommend vitamin A.

From the beginnings of my differentness, I remember
    doctors, students, therapists
measuring my head,
the tightness of my muscles,
the tracking of my eyes,
the dysfunctions of my stomach.
Some were stiff and cold,
others blessedly kind,
others not acknowledging I understood every word
they said,
so freely did they label me retarded,
or some other variant,
equally untrue.
These my parents left,
tight-lipped and coiled
for research,
telling me always they knew I was there
inside,

and somehow we would find each other,
connect,
the way they could with the sisters and brother
following after me.

Still there are questions beyond questions
about etiologies of this behavior
or that,
each potential answer unfolding
into a deeper question
even more mystifying.
Now I am not only subject,
but researcher,
giving valuable feedback
on treatment results,
sharing the inside view,
learning from the outside,
not startlingly different in appearance or habits
from that little boy so willingly labeled.
But now I can type thoughts, questions,
responses,
enter discussions on Shakespeare and
algebra,
vote, give opinions on government actions.
Now my mind is free, is free
to join with your mind and hammer out
solutions,
or ponder new theories while
watching my fingers,
doing nothing
down in my room.

Hearthside

The flames are wild like tigers
or balls of orange
trying to tumble around each other,
then vanishing up up up
to be replaced by more
dashes of flames,
and crackling of wood,
and smell of ashes,
like strong incense.
Now it is dying
and glowing coals
remind me of sleep.

Listener

I have seen the photographs
a hundred times
of a blond boy stretching small hands across
a keyboard.
I have heard the stories
of how that three-year-old,
who couldn't yet walk,
clung to the piano for balance,
happily plunking out notes
on his journey up and down
the registers.
They say I began by banging,
then gradually moved on to octaves and chords
the local piano teacher said
I was too young
to hear.
They tell me the old upright
was missing a front panel
and when they covered the keys,
I played the hammers,
so driven was I
to make music.

I remember the elation
of discovering sound,
of producing combinations of
pitches,
listening to overtones,

like waves pulsing through
my ears,
studying the shapes of the tones
in my mind
like a science,
examining, analyzing
phenomena.

They tell me I have perfect pitch
as I match the hum of the dryer
to a white key.
I know the names of the sounds now,
every note of a suite
or a sonata
my palsied hands long
to play.

I have compared the pianos
of different churches,
contrasting the timbre of a Kawai,
with a Brinkerhoff,
a Baldwin,
a Selmer,
exhilarating in their differences.

My grandma's organ,
like my keyboard,
lulls me with its endless
fascinating variations of
sound effects
and rhythm.

I lose myself in this Disneyland
of delight,
listening, adjusting,
refining,
until I have orchestrated
the perfect combination
which I play
over and over again,
saturating my senses,
content.

Perhaps for you
the hum of a vacuum cleaner
is a nuisance
to be ignored
or forgotten.
For me, life is a living symphony
of sound,
each infinitely satisfying
and curious,
worthy of attention
and remembrance.

Frustration

I stare at them every day,
Checking to make sure they haven't moved—
Mirror, bed, keyboard, dresser, closet.
They're all in place,
All helping my life seem attractive,
Orderly, safe.

You see, we know every detail
In the pictures of our minds,
Thousand of details to sort out,
Keep organized,
Like an eternal spring cleaning
To keep us sane.
The number of bricks in a building,
The position of windows and doors,
Trees, flowers, grass,
Changes, adaptations, changes again.

People think savant skills make life easier.
Exhausting is my word for the struggle
Of overload.
Screening out details gives your life focus,
A chance to zoom in for a time.
I'm looking for needles in
Gigantic haystacks
And it isn't getting any easier,

So playing my nailing-down-each-thing-in-the-room
    game
Isn't a game,
It's the only way I can sleep.

Beloved One

I do not know how I knew
from the very beginning, He was there
great hands gloriously holding my life,
little that I was.
In the confusion of lights and overwhelming
sounds, He was there.
I felt Him around me, crooning His love.
I heard Him in my mother's lullabies.
I heard Him when I couldn't speak to anyone else,
though they all spoke to me.
I talked to Him in my desperate
loneliness, and his words kept me
strong.
I saw Him in the eyes of volunteers,
in their patience and laughter as they
moved my body.
I saw His angels around me one night
in a scary place.

He is my comforter
when no one else has time,
my encourager in discouragement,
my song when I am out of melodies.
He is my healer,
the healer for now and in heaven
when He tells me we will
run together.
He is my God.

I cannot be anything but His child,
for He is my life.
Love surrounding me,
all my days and beyond.
I love you.

Reverie

I dream of shovels and pitchforks
penetrating rich black loam,
tillers churning through virgin sod,
wheelbarrows trundling manure,
tiny seeds laid in careful rows,
throughly covered,
sprinklers spinning their watery tunes
out over thirsty ground,
seedlings pushing up into
blazing sunshine,
stretching, reaching, unfurling
leaves, flowers, fruit,
scarlet globes splitting on
laden stems,
verdant peas hanging in graceful company,
shimmering cornsilks drying into
clumps of brown,
warted squash piled together with pumpkins,
striped green and yellow and orange,
riotous vines thick with
glossy cucumbers,
buckets of potatoes resting
near hollowed ground.

I dream as the snow falls silently, thickly,
shrouding the earth in white.

Encounter

"Answer!"
I told my mouth
but the message
froze,
while seconds dragged into minutes
and the restless woman
said fast
goodbyes
swiftly dashing
assumptions of
intelligence
behind her.

Words are
power;
speechlessness,
an endless abyss;
garbled speech,
a target for dishonor;
persistent rotten storytelling,
a huge annoyance;
boring tapes that
demean
my image.

You whose language flows
coherently,
whose ideas sparkle like wine

on the tongue,
remember your gift
and use it well,
for me.

Initiation

Growing didn't stop them
from trying to understand
this strange older brother
they inherited,
normal to them at first,
normal, as hours of therapy
unfolded before their infant eyes,
a motley parade of people,
hands that moved,
swung, rolled, stroked,
voices that read countless books,
sung crazy songs,
all reaching out to me,
my sisters, my brother.
When did they realize
that other families didn't have
an automatic playgroup,
a gymnasium in the basement,
and tutors coming every night?
Was it the first Saturday at a friend's house
when nobody rocked
or talked to himself,
or the first time somebody said,
"Your brother's a retard,"
and they didn't know how to answer?
Sometimes they grumble,
but look beyond embarassments,
and wish with me that autism would be over.

We form bridges into each other's lives
and find out we aren't so different
after all.

The Daring Times
for Betsy

The whole fun thing about life
is the minutes,
seemingly wasted,
in the contentment of love.
Love, with all grace and reason,
not love that uses and runs away,
but love that waits,
and holds my hand,
and cries with me,
even when my tears are hidden
beneath autistic faces.
This is contentment:
to be loved beneath the rotten talk,
and the waving,
and the rocking,
and the grinding teeth,
and the gradually aggravating testing garbage,
to be loved beneath it all,
and in spite of it all,
and through it all.
In those moments I can go on without fear,
for love is my armor,
and you are my standard bearer,
my contented, loving friend.

Distant Pleasure

Nine bundles of fur tumbling
out of the barn,
racing pell-mell to surround us
on the back steps,
short-haired, long-haired,
yapping, play-fighting
progeny,
sired by three different
fathers,
jumble of multiculturalism,
Elsie's pride.

"Puppies! Puppies! Puppies!"
my sisters called
while I steeled myself for
the invasion of licking,
restless bodies,
the girls' definition of heaven,
my struggle with
suffocation,
pushing away nails, teeth, tongues,
weight,
until they gathered on
my sisters' laps
and I could just
grin
at nine inquisitive pairs of eyes
staring
at me.

The Banquet

I have to hear the words.
The lines you decipher so easily become
swirls of pain for me.
Never think reading is a bore,
a hardship foisted on you
by difficult teachers.
It is freedom,
doorways into a hundred thousand different lives.
You turn the page and life
is there for you;
I pick out words and phrases,
wishing it didn't have to hurt,
fall apart before my eyes.
I wait for loving voices to bring me
the stories,
so my mind can feast again.

In Deep

I free my hands from their
plodding trance,
in the water,
where they plunge through resistance
and swirl back in glistening circles
of rainbow light.
My legs, too, pump water past
and around,
not uselessly,
moving me in directions
planned
and reached.
Here I am a force,
achieving a propulsion, grace, rhythm,
each movement,
verse in a water poem
I am writing around me.
Here I dance
unassisted,
pleasure in every muscle and pore;
here only in harmony with
this physique I call home,
satiated in freedom,
while terror falls away,
daring to descend,
then burst up through the surface,
laughing.
Here I awaken to life's
possibilities.

Inevitable Results

They are my hope and my doom,
These things that occupy my mind with such ferocity
That there is no room for anything else.
You call them interests; I call them obsessions.
They bless my life with excitement,
Curse my life with their endless repetition.
Without obsessions, nothing would draw me into
Your world;
With them, I am bound into a frightening cycle
Of Madness.

Historians say Einstein was autistic,
A genius.
They say he was antisocial,
A misfit.
Was his mind so full of theories and experiments
That he could hardly breathe?

Windmills, water, windows, bridges,
Music, lights, numbers, countries . . .
My list goes on and on.
Sometimes I wish they would all
Go away so I could make
Friends.
Will people call me a genius
Someday or just a fool
In love with weird things?
Make my obsessions worth something, Lord
Or I will always be alone.

Solace

They told me we were moving
again,
not fully comprehending how long
it takes me
to feel safe
in strange overwhelming
walls.
But,
they told me I'd get used to it
slowly.
The house was old,
needed work.
We unwrapped
its tired surface
one layer at a time.
Men plastered;
we painted,
sanded,
stained,
until one day it gleamed inside
and I could sleep in
my room.

Two long narrow windows
reminded me of I's,
sentinels,
keeping watch over
my slumbering form.

Through one I glimpsed
a pleasure-view
of lake and sky,
always changing,
reassuringly the same.

I watched eagles swoop down
after dozing fish
and pelicans fly by
on their way
to unknown lakes.
I heard sparrows, finches,
woodpeckers,
a hundred birds twittering
at once,
the lapping of the water,
the haunting call of a loon.

My sanctuary
from the endlessness of
human disorientation,
I savored stolen time
by the stirring curtain,
refreshed
my scattered nerves,
found solace
for my spirit.
Then,
they told me we were moving
again.

Free-Fall

Time is the best facilitator of my life.
Time unfolds my fear,
allowing my slow fingers to have their say.
In the hurry-up of this world,
people like me get left behind.
Conversations are about speed,
schedules about regimenting every minute.
I cannot jump in fast enough before
they are off to the next topic.
When I type, how agonizing is the wait
between the beginning and the end!
Sometimes I slow down and stop,
just to watch people stiffen and get restless.
They probably pity me,
the poor one-fingered communicator,
but I pity them too.
I live in free-fall; they are taking the Concorde.
Which of us has the best view?

Mirror

His name was Dan.
We met in our church one afternoon,
his mother clutching his homemade wooden board.
Dan was 18; I was only 11.
But we were alike inside;
I could feel it.
He was the first person with autism
I had ever met.

I was new to this typing stuff; Dan was a pro.
He started the conversation;
I answered timidly.
Don't you wonder how it was for us,
feeling out the autism in each other?
We had both inhabited the silence of our selves
for a long lonely time.
All around us had been other, foreign.
Now we had found mirrors of ourselves.
Better yet, we were both daring to join
This crazy confusing chaos
people called reality.

Dan moved away. We never write.
I hope his journey is going well.

All Circuits Are Busy

Begin at the beginning
then continue on to the next page,
sequentially adding to your mind
building blocks of knowledge,
kindergarden, first grade, on and on,
high school, college, graduate school,
making you a learner for life.

We don't follow patterns,
piling fact on fact;
all senses pull information into
overloaded circuits,
plethora of puzzling sensations,
ideas, mystery,
formulas found out by
befuddled ponderers.
Out of conscious thought
our stories are written;
consciously recognizing our ideas
as we read them,
foreign,
yet completely familiar,
in and out of the shadows of our genius?
Confusion?

Somehow in the center
we search for the why and how,
mathematical order,

mystical meanings,
survival,
security,
sanity,
somewhere to store it all,
study it all,
share what we can,
making us librarians for life.

GFCF Trust

Life is better for me now,
Better than a year ago.
The stream of opiates in my brain
May have slowed, even stopped.
Now I have to wait for the residues
To leave my body.
We scrutinize every label,
Checking for every crumb of gluten,
Every drop of casein.
I crunch down my rice bread
And almond butter happily,
Knowing that next year
Will probably be better yet.
Maybe my brain will stop
Its persistent repetition
And give me peace.

My stomach never hurts now;
My headaches are mostly gone.
I am hopeful for second chances
And healing.

Lost Friend

She looked like a blaze
of flame,
amber eyes singed by
burnt orange hair,
eager, hungry,
regal even then,
head inside a dead cow's udder,
putrid, feasting with
brothers and sisters,
until the embarrassed farmer
lured her away with
dog food,
and we brought her
home.

Elsie
the queen,
the bear,
the guardian,
stretches on the porch with
nursing cats,
scampers over fields
and under bridges,
chasing pheasants, rabbits, ducks,
whimpers her welcome in
rolled-over surrender,
and somehow she knows
I am different,

other,
for never will she come,
not even when I call,
never will she come
to me.

Daring Tears

My grandpa died last night.
The family cried in grief and shock,
Holding each other in one group hug
While I sat by our space heater
And stared into the darkness.
I was crying inside too,
But no one knew
Because my face rarely shows
The struggles of my heart.

I remember one day when my emotions got through,
When my loneliness reached a point of desperation
And tears came pouring out.
Mom was there to hold me
Until my sobbing stilled.
Comfort is a privilege
But without communication
What chance is there of comfort?

Later last night Mom got out the board
And let me share my pain,
Hugged me in spite of my stiff response,
Reached into my heart.
Never never think you understand
How we autistic people feel.
Underneath the giggles, we may be
Dying inside.
Thank God there is someone in my life
Who listens.

The Search

Ghana caught my attention first,
Panama, Zambia, Corsica,
Then Kayla, Jessica, Erica, Elena,
Iowa, South Dakota,
And best of all,
Mozzarella,
Lovely sibilance of sounds.

Trunk, shrug, shrunk,
Deep in the o of your lips,
Indescribably delicious
To taste.

Today,
A constant reminder of
The fresh joy of now,
This minute,
Gifted celebration time,
Soon to pass.

Hunting new delights to savor
In word stew,
Wrap in phrases round each other,
Blending sound and meaning,
Meaning and sound,

Until together they become
Nourishment for your spirit,
Playtime for your mind,
Satisfaction for your heart.
Enjoy!

Tradition

October meant trail-walking
at St. John's,
a mile or so around the lake
and back,
through blazing trees dressed
for winter's coming,
up and down leaf-strewn paths,
underlaced by tree roots,
occasional stones,
fallen twigs.
The tree roots were my downfall,
transforming my ungraceful lope
into sudden sprawls,
the tree roots,
and the distance.
Fatigued by constant vigilance
I gladly rested by the old stone church,
halfway point,
holy ground.

The first year Mom practically carried me
the last quarter mile,
as tired whiners fought over
paths not chosen.
The next year she brought tandem
and dog,
but the tandem's chain slipped,
and brakes failed,

sending my sister hurtling
down the slope.
Dogs and bikes were
against the rules,
they informed us,
so I was back to loping
and sprawling.

By now October trail-walking
was tradition,
eagerly anticipated,
lovingly recounted,
not to be missed.
Tramping trails together,
gulping huge lungfuls of
fresh fall air,
watching squirrels gather
winter's hoard,
listening, above all, listening,
to frogs, ducks, silence,
these attractions drew us back
like migrating geese to
a favorite shelter,
like family,
glad to be alive.

The Funny Thing About These People

Arresting history and reading the evidence,
We are nickel-and-dime people to world normals,
Found, when wonder at differences is low,
And acceptance incomprehensible.
Autism, awesome, they go together fashionably,
Wasting more is easy, digging out potential hard,
Better than tying up, holding down, ignoring.

That is the answer to isolation:
Wanting to search the talent
And find heart's treasure.

Reflection

The days sweep by, each one a chasing
After the world.
What new skills must I master
To join the ranks of society?
Senior years are exciting,
Disconcerting, too short.
We are all trying to figure out
Our contribution to life.
Where do we make our mark?
We may feel worthless,
A speck in a vast galaxy of beings,
But God sees otherwise.
What would this world be like
Without Charles Schultz
Or Billy Graham,
Julia Roberts, Mother Teresa
Or Shakespeare?
Each of them began
As a confused 19-year old
Trying to find his or her way.
Can we walk our path above the noise
Of jeerers and disbelievers?
Especially me?

Anticipation

Mouth giggling heart fluttering
Palms sweating upper lip tingling
Clock ticking far too slowly for decency
When will it arrive?
The cool calm of my afterschool time,
Blue room, no flickering lights,
Trees, wind, an occasional faraway train,
The loosening of my tight nerves,
Quiet rustling in the moonlight,
Family voices,
The closest this autistic body gets
To peace.

Appreciation

I love the passion of notes
thundering up and down the octaves,
the weaving together of melodies
and countermelodies,
the tremolo of a violin,
the thump of a deep bass drum,
the shimmering of brass.
Music is the regulator of my nervous system,
the shelter for my frazzled mind,
the delight of my heart.
It makes life bearable on some days,
fabulous on others.
They say we autistic people
are gifted musically.
Actually I'm just in love with notes.
Someday I will write a symphony
from the chords I have collected
in my mind.
Someday, just for fun.
In the meantime, I will listen
and listen, and listen,
'Til I am filled to the brim
with joy.

Inertia

Spring bides its time;
its gray mornings drift into
gray afternoons,
occasionally lifting
the cover of clouds,
sending shafts of sunlight
onto sodden ground
where robins cluster,
cats wander,
new lambs bleat for
woolly ewes.
Yesterday I noticed
a sprinkling of green
over a bleak pasture,
today only more gray,
silence,
waiting.
Living on this hill I watch
for signs of growth
yet spring
bides its time.

Outsider

We are drawn to them
like a drowning man to a life preserver,
like a panting runner to water,
like a fisherman to his favorite lake,
drawn to the women in our lives.

Yes, I notice too,
their kindness,
their softness,
the way their hair shines in the sunlight,
the music in their laughter,
the shape of their movements,
the sympathy in their glances,
I, behind my curtain of behaviors,
I notice too.

I danced with silken maidens
at prom this year,
in tux, bedecked with honor,
I moved to startling rhythms.
I watched couples wander,
arms entwined,
while music throbbed its love song
and wished for dates and kisses,
love for me and all my brothers,
love that reaches past our barriers.
We need it too.

Request

This is the beginning of a new millenium
Where all of us need to belong in schools,
Jobs, colleges, communities.
We need to make our presence known.
I know we are unpredictable,
Embarrassing, not always beautiful.
We spoil the TV images of
Perfection and riches.
Pictures of poor children in slums intrude
On your consciousness.
You can push them away.
But we are here in every neighborhood,
Wanting to be welcomed into
This life we share together.
Will you invite us in?

Sunday Morning

Greatness untamable,
we call to You,
needy,
lifting our faces from the
minutiae of our minds
to the balm of Your presence,
blanketing our sadness.
Wealth, power, fame, security play
with our vanities,
but You, O Most High Inconceivable God,
meet us here in this room,
with gladness pouring from your eyes,
forgiveness granted,
grace slipping into the recesses
of our fractured hearts
and we sing! we sing!
then quietly slip
back to earth's boundenness,
carrying the sweetness,
the whisper of Your love,
like starlight,
leading the way.

In Limbo

Sheep sidle through my dreams,
Bleating, black-hoofed, sharp-nosed sheep,
Thundering staccatos over our porch,
Startling hissing cats,
Nibbling gigantic spreading thistles,
Following back to curly back,
Right and left around the pen,
Seeking entrance, finding none,
Scurrying mounds of wool and will.

Plotting escape, they searched for exits,
Jumping fences built too low,
Squeezing through gaps
To gallivant and caper,
Undeterred in tasting freedom,
Finding freedom strange and bitter,
Racing back to fence and shelter,
Panicked, lost, demanding boundaries,
Frantic flock of wool and will.

Nightmares!
I am daring, daring...
Running home to prison's safety,
Pushing out through hated barriers,
Trying newness on for pleasure,
Thinking, trusting strange beginnings,
Stretching past old haunting habits,
Lost in places with no limits,
Fighting hard through work and will.

Tracings

Fresh air seems like the answer
to the question of what to do with
an obsessing being.
Walks always help.
Energy levels rise;
scenery becomes more enticing than
the mantra of favorite stories,
the allurement of waving fingers.
Of course, there are always electrical poles
lined up like giant toothpicks,
humming,
like lost bees.
Poles can bring the mind
new absorbing questions
about distance, angle and height,
mathematical calculations
to figure and refigure again.
Trees are a different mystery—
bare, dressed, or dying,
trunks, solid foundations for
songs of spreading branches,
their swaying melody
whispery-soft.
I have studied trees
for as long as I can remember
and still do not understand
      their why in embracing
the sky.

Grasses rippling in the wind
focus and refocus,
blur of patterns, texures,
population of thousands,
each sprightly blade losing itself
in the green.
Grass is for walking through,
pulling at, tasting,
trailing through ready hands.
Sun in every position, or
occasionally, the moon,
surrounded by the appropriate colors,
rings, clouds.
I see them in my periphery,
too awe-inspiring in their royal cycles
for traditional viewing;
I bask in their benevolence.
Then home to fireside and rest
for wobbly legs,
brief respite from the body's
frenzied habits,
new images to store
in mind's expanding maze,
a taste of tranquility
held in memory,
until the next time
the question emerges.

Graduation

for Mom

Great friend, listener,
Divider of my shroud of fear,
To you the words are given
That no one else knows are there,
For in perfect relaxation they flow like a river of escape,
Of connection, of joy.
Long you battled my defenses,
The gobbledygook of a frightened mind,
Reassuring me that the words could proceed unimpeded
Through practice and trust.
Eventually you calmed my spirit enough
That my mind could direct
My hand,
And the words,
Triumphant,
Blaze their message
From ignominious disability
To honored academia.

This I celebrate today—
Tassel hanging, robe swishing,
Marching with measured steps into the ceremony.
With honors
They tell the world,
While onlookers silently wonder,
But you and I know the journey we have traveled
Together.

So great friend, listener,
Divider of my shroud of fear,
I carry this diploma for all the years
You sought me.
Now my words can comfort you.
Listen.

Inquiry

Could it be that all this aberration,
wandering eyes,
painfully-stiff limbs,
delayed speech,
garbled everything
is the result of mercury
resting in my brain cells,
inhibiting my enzymes
from all this world considers
normal?

We are the pioneers,
weekly pulling micrograms of metal
from our bodies,
building up immunity,
flushing out toxins,
measuring our progress,
waiting for signs of change
however
infinitesimal.

I grow gladder, stronger,
more at rest,
each week a lessening of the torture
I have called life,
a welcoming of new sensations, perceptions.
I beg for continuation,
another cycle of detoxification,

perhaps another cell waking up
to functions interrupted,
to life in all its fullness.
I pray I am not too late to discover
the man I could have been.

Endeavor

Noticing reasons for staying connected
dares farther than I have
stirred myself
until now,
for winging back into my refuge of
sameness and private mutterings
is my daily, hourly sojourn,
pleasing my overturning,
worn nervous system
by focus on a narrow theme,
a word,
nothingness.

Now, some of the tension is
dissipating,
some distorted visual images
piecing themselves into
semi-complete wholes,
some tingling discomfort relaxing
into waves of normalcy,
now a hug,
a gesture of delight,
not repulsing stiffness.

We have a long journey still,
I and the companion of
my descent
and slow return.

She holds her breath as she faces me
across a tower of blocks,
baby play,
unmastered, but now
a second chance.
I place a tenth cube
atop its wavering foundation
then release my grasp.
The edifice stands.
We high-five and cheer
such paltry success,
tiny victory.

No choice beyond
this faltering, hope-laden retracing of
missed development
lies in my daily path.
I can study classical literature,
but I must,
I must study
the painful, tentative melding of
eyes and hands
in useful work,
else I will always wait
for assistance
in a time when conquering
is synonymous
with competence.

So I continue,
daring eyes to focus well,
the beads in one hand to connect with

the cord in the other,
to slide down gracefully,
all twenty-eight,
swinging the colorful pendulum
of my progress,
a grand hurrah
in the face of my future.

Why I Drag Maps Around The House

If I could be anything,
I'd be an explorer
with vistas of unending
beauty
before me,
and memories of
engrossing experiences
behind me.
I'd board trains, planes, boats;
climb, hike, swim,
discover
all I could in one lifetime;
study history, ecology,
archaeology;
understand the why's and hows
of each mountain
and valley
and the life teeming
around it.
I'd photograph and write about
my treasures,
sharing the joy.
Then I'd die,
content.
They'd bury my bones
on top of
the highest mountain
I'd ever climbed,

and my spirit would rest with
Creator God.
If I could be anything…